SURVIVE ALIVE

FIRE AND COOKING

Neil Champion

amicus

Published by Amicus
P.O. Box 1329
Mankato, MN 56002

Printed in the United States of America, at Corporate Graphics
in North Mankato, Minnesota

Library of Congress Cataloging-in-Publication Data
Champion, Neil.
  Fire and cooking / by Neil Champion.
      p. cm. -- (Survive alive)
  Includes index.
  Summary: "Gives essential survival tips for building a fire and cooking in
the wild, including information on different kinds of fires. Also discusses
how to know what to cook and utensils to use"--Provided by publisher.
  ISBN 978-1-60753-039-8 (library binding)
  1. Camping--Juvenile literature. 2. Campfires--Juvenile literature. 3.
Survival skills--Juvenile literature. I. Title.
  GV191.7.C46 2010
  796.54--dc22

                                                          2010001626

Created by Appleseed Editions Ltd.
Designed and illustrated by Guy Callaby
Edited by Stephanie Turnbull
Picture research by Su Alexander

Picture acknowledgements

Page 3 D Hurst/Alamy Page 4 Gary Cook/Alamy; 5l Colin Harris/LightTouch Images/
Alamy, r FrancieZant/Alamy; 6 Roger Bamber/Alamy; 7 Edward Parke/Alamy; 8 Arturs
Stalidzans/Alamy; 9 Charles O Cecil/Alamy; 10 David Forster/Alamy; 12 AfriPics.com/
Alamy; 13 Niall Benvie/Alamy; 14 Roger Bamber/Alamy; 16 Blickwinkel/Alamy; 17 ESA
Hiltula CC/Alamy; 18 D Hurst/Alamy; 19 Celia Mannings/Alamy; 20 Nick Hanna/Alamy;
21l Dor Posner, r Antje Schulte-Scandinavia/Alamy; 22 PCL/Alamy; 23t All Canada
Photos/Alamy, b INSADCO Photography/Alamy; 24 Maximilian Weinzierl/Alamy;
25 David Kilpatrick/Alamy; 26 Karen Kasmauski/Science Faction/Corbis; 27 James
Marshall/Corbis

Front cover: Bill Bachman/Alamy

DAD0038
32010

9 8 7 6 5 4 3 2 1

Contents

Fire for Survival

Imagine being lost in a wild forest as a storm rages. It's too dark to see properly and you're tired, cold, and soaked to the skin. You find a cave to shelter in and curl up on the damp ground, shivering. You need a fire and you need it fast. Would you know what to do?

A Vital Skill

Being able to make a fire is an essential survival skill. A fire provides warmth, light, and protection from animals and insects. It lets you cook food, boil water, and dry out clothes. If you're tired, lonely, or injured, a fire can help cheer you up. In an emergency, a fire could even make the difference between life and death.

▼ *Having a good campfire makes you feel safer and therefore more comfortable in the wild.*

Be Prepared

If you're planning an expedition into wild country, you have to be well prepared. What kind of food will you need to take and how will you cook it? Will you carry a portable stove or make a campfire? What will you need for fuel? Be sure to think all these things through before you set off.

◀ *If you'll be camping in a snowy place, you must be able to find dry wood to burn.*

▲ *Even the largest backpacks have limited space for food and fuel. You need to leave room for other essentials, too!*

Traveling Light

If your trip is only a few days, you can carry all your food and fuel. However, if you plan to be outdoors for a week or more, you may need to find extra food and fuel. This is why it's useful to know how to find them in the wild. If you have these skills, you can carry less on your back from the start.

TRUE SURVIVAL STORY

CHRIS is a hiker who was once camping in the Sierra Nevadas. He set off on a short walk wearing just a t-shirt and shorts, carrying some food and a small wood-powered camp stove. Then things went wrong. It started to rain and Chris slipped and broke his leg. He crawled under a tree, put some twigs in his stove, and lit it. The small fire gave off enough heat to dry his clothes and keep him warm. As the rain turned to snow, Chris huddled by his stove all night. The next day, he made crutches out of branches and started back to his camp, often stopping to light the stove and warm himself. After another night outdoors, he finally made it back. He is sure that the fire saved his life.

Fire Basics

Fires need three things to burn: fuel, **oxygen**, and heat. There are many kinds of fuel, including wood, coal, gasoline, and paraffin. Oxygen is in the air around us. Heat is what gets the fire going in the first place. This may come from matches, a steel and **flint** kit, or some other method of fire lighting (see pages 10–13).

Finding Fuel

If your fire runs out of fuel, it will go out—so make sure you have a good fuel supply. If you're using wood, find plenty of dead branches. Freshly-cut **green**, or live, wood contains a lot of water, so it won't burn well. You must also make sure the wood is dry. Any wood lying on the ground may be damp, so look for dead branches on standing trees.

▼ Gather plenty of fuel so you can keep your fire burning for a long time.

Wood for Burning

Not all wood burns in the same way, so it makes sense to learn to identify different types of trees and know which to look for. For example, ash and beech wood burn very well and give off plenty of light and heat. Birch wood is also good, but it burns very quickly. Wood from chestnut trees may crackle and spit, so be careful. Avoid alder, elder, and lime wood, as they give off lots of smoke and very little heat.

Smoky Fires

Smoke is a mixture of gases and **tar** from wood. Once a fire is very hot, the gases and tar burn away, which is why a fire is usually smokier when it is first lit. If your wood is damp, then the fire takes longer to get going, so it will be smoky for longer. Smoke **pollutes** the air, so try to avoid it as much as possible.

▲ *Dry, dead branches from this beech tree would burn very well.*

1. *Newly-lit fires always produce smoke, especially if wood is green.*

2. *When the fire is burning well, there should be much less smoke.*

3. *When the fire burns down to **embers**, it hardly smokes at all.*

A Good Air Supply

Build your fire in an open area so that plenty of air can get to it. However, make sure it isn't in a windy place, otherwise you won't feel the heat—and the fire may get blown out. To avoid this, make the fire in a dip in the ground or near a natural windbreak, such as a large rock.

Beware!

Never make a fire inside your tent or shelter. Not only could bedding and other materials catch on fire, but fire uses oxygen from the air to burn, leaving less for you to breathe. A fire also gives off smoke and **carbon monoxide**, which are dangerous to inhale.

▼ *Try warming a shelter with hot stones in a can. Put the can in a place where you won't touch it by mistake and burn yourself.*

Preparing a Fire

Before making a fire, you need to choose a suitable site and prepare it well. First, find a dry, clear area that is not too close to your shelter. Brush away leaves, grass, and other vegetation for at least 6.5 ft. (2 m) around, so the fire doesn't spread. Make sure there are no overhanging branches from trees or bushes that could catch fire.

▲ *The dry, spongy inside layer of a bracket fungus like this one makes good tinder because it lights easily.*

Fuel Types

To start a fire, you need three types of fuel: tinder, kindling, and the main fuel. Tinder is the material that catches a spark and starts to glow. Kindling gets the flames burning and the main fuel keeps the fire burning for a long time. Collect plenty of each material before you light the fire and make sure they are dry. Never underestimate how much tinder and kindling you will need, especially if you're trying to start a fire in wet or windy weather. If you run out, your fire will never get going!

1. *Tinder can be any soft, fluffy, or fine material that will catch fire easily, such as shredded paper, moss, seed heads, or crumbly, rotten wood.*

2. *Kindling is usually made up of small twigs and sticks. It should be thin enough to catch fire from the tinder, but thick enough to produce flames and heat to light the main fuel.*

3. *The main fuel should be medium and large sticks, plus logs to add once the fire is burning well.*

Knife Skills

If you have a good camping knife, you can use it to help create extra fuel. For example, you could look for bark that has peeled off a tree, roll it up and slice it into small coils to use as tinder. You could also make feather sticks by carefully cutting very thin, curly shavings at the end of kindling sticks. These feathery ends will help the sticks catch fire easily.

DID YOU KNOW?
*In the past, American Indians who lived on treeless **prairies** used dried buffalo dung as fuel for fire.*

◀ *Birch trees have lots of loose, papery bark that peels off easily. Removing a lot of bark from a living tree can damage it, so take only what you really need.*

TRUE SURVIVAL STORY

FRANCIS YOUNGHUSBAND was an explorer who made a perilous journey across the Himalayan Mountains in 1887. This included a six-hour climb down a sheer, icy **precipice**, followed by a long, exhausting trek through deep snow. Finally, late at night, Younghusband and his guides found a dry place to shelter under rocks. There was no wood for a fire, but they were able to find some grass, which they managed to light. It was a small fire, but enough to keep them alive and warm through the long night.

Lighting a Fire

Once you're sure you've collected plenty of fuel—enough to last a whole night if necessary—then you're ready to light your fire. For this you need a spark that will light your tinder. The simplest and easiest way to do this is with a match.

DID YOU KNOW?
You should never carry loose matches in your pockets, as they could be struck accidentally and severely burn you. Keep them in a waterproof container.

Vital Supplies

Matches are an essential item to take with you into the wild. Buy waterproof matches that will strike even when wet or try waterproofing ordinary matches by dipping the heads into melted wax. This cools to form a simple waterproof coating. When you use one of the matches, the action of striking it will knock the wax off.

▲ *Feathery curls of wood light very easily with a match. Always be careful that you don't burn your fingers, and don't throw the match away until you're sure it's out.*

Getting Started

The larger your matches are, the more time you have to transfer the flame to your tinder. Alternatively, try lighting a long paper or cardboard **taper** with your match, then use this to light the tinder.

1. Put the tinder on the ground and prop kindling around it. Leave enough space to get your match to the tinder.

2. Once the tinder is burning, the flames and heat will rise and light the kindling. Add small pieces of your main fuel supply as the fire gets going.

Add bigger pieces of wood as the fire grows.

Steel and Flint

A good backup to matches is a steel and flint kit. These kits contain a curved piece of steel and a sharp flint that you can use to make sparks.

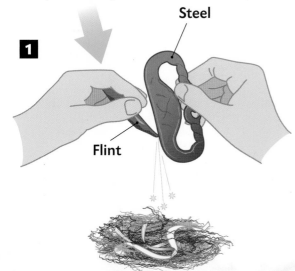

Steel

Flint

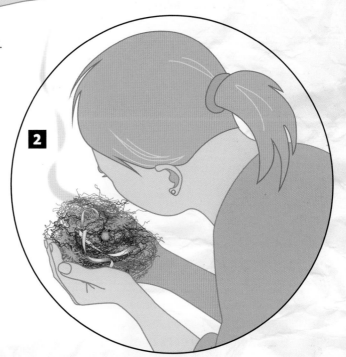

1. Hold the steel over your tinder. Strike the flint against the steel in a downward motion. Sparks will fly down toward the tinder.

2. When a spark falls on the tinder and a glowing red ember appears, blow on it steadily to help it catch fire. You could hold the tinder up to give it more air.

When the tinder starts to burn, carefully put it under your kindling.

More Fire-Making Skills

If you find yourself stranded in the wild without matches or a steel and flint kit, you can try using some ancient fire-making skills. They take a lot of patience and practice, but they might make all the difference in an emergency survival situation.

DID YOU KNOW?
It's hard to light fires in damp, steamy jungles. Native people in the South Pacific use a **fire piston** that creates sparks.

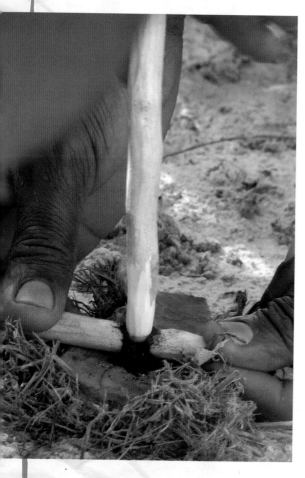

Friction Sticks

In the past, people such as American Indians used **friction** sticks to make fire. It takes a lot of skill! You need a smooth, straight stick, a flat piece of wood, and a knife or sharp stone for carving.

1. *Make a hollow in the wood, big enough for the end of the stick to fit in. Carve a notch from the hole to the edge of the wood. This is your fireboard.*

2. *Put some tinder under the fireboard to catch sparks, then spin the stick very quickly in the hollow. After a while, smoke will form.*

3. *Eventually, the two pieces of wood rubbing together will generate enough heat to produce an ember that falls through the notch and onto your tinder.*

▲ **Bushmen** in the Kalahari Desert, Botswana, show how a friction stick works. This method works best in hot places, where wood is very dry and ignites quickly.

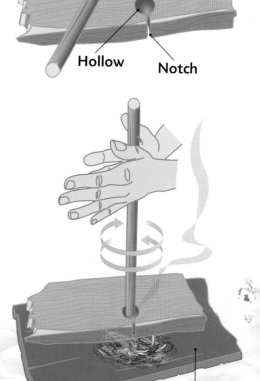

Friction stick | Fireboard
Hollow | Notch

Bark to rest on

Adding a Bow

If you make a wooden bow with a string, you can use it to spin the stick instead of using your hands. It's a more effective method, but it takes longer to prepare.

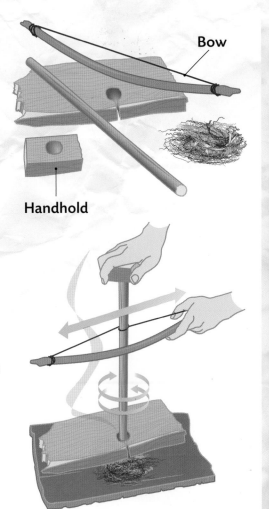

Bow

Handhold

1. *Tie string, cord, or even a shoelace to a curved stick to make a bow. You also need a block of wood with a hollow in it to use as a handhold for your friction stick.*

2. *Twist the string around the stick and move the bow back and forth quickly so that the stick spins. Use the handhold to keep the stick in place. If it helps, hold the fireboard in place with your foot.*

Fire with a Lens

If you have a magnifying glass, you can try to concentrate the sun's rays onto tinder. Eventually the tinder will start to smolder. Blow gently on it to create a small flame, then gradually add more tinder. This method is also used by polar explorers to create fire using a lens carved from ice.

▶ *Making fire with a lens can be tricky—and of course it only works on a sunny day!*

Types of Fires

DID YOU KNOW?
On damp ground, you need to build a dry platform for your fire first. Use criss-crossed logs, flat stones, or strips of dry bark.

You can build your fire in several different ways, depending on what you need it for and how long you want it to last. It may be just for cooking or to light and heat your whole camp. You may only need it for a few hours or you may want it to burn all night and the next day, too. Here are some common fire designs.

Tepee Fire

The simplest design is a **tepee** fire, as shown on page 11. Start with a bundle of tinder. Prop small kindling sticks around it in a cone shape. Then add larger sticks. Don't add too many large sticks at once, or you may smother the fire.

Star Fire

If you need your fire to last for a long time, build it in a star shape. It won't give out a lot of heat or light, but it will last as long as you want it to and not use too much fuel.

1. *Make a small ball of tinder. Light it, and then add small kindling sticks.*

2. *When the fire is burning well, put six or eight medium-sized main fuel branches in the fire in a star shape. As the ends burn down, move the branches nearer to the fire.*

◀ *A tepee fire burns quickly and brightly and gives off plenty of warmth and light.*

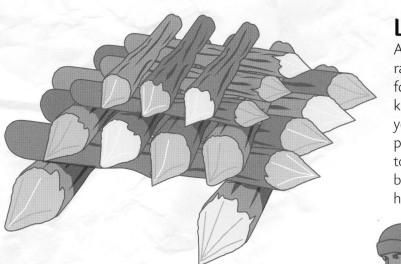

Log Cabin Fire

A log cabin fire creates lots of embers rather than big flames, so it is good for cooking on. Start with tinder and kindling in the middle and build up your logs around it in a criss-cross pattern. Once the fire is going, try to keep the shape by adding larger branches and logs, depending on how long you need the fire to last.

Keep the Heat

If your fire is for keeping you warm, you can make it more efficient by building a wall of logs or rocks near the fire. This will reflect heat back toward you and stop your back from getting too cold. Another option is to wrap a sleeping bag or blanket around you to keep your back warm.

TRUE SURVIVAL STORY

CHRIS KAVANAUGH was a member of an archaeological team visiting an island off the coast of California in 2001. The boat carrying their supplies never arrived and they were stranded for three days. Two men had brought machetes and were soon hard at work cutting wood for a fire. Kavanaugh had a smarter idea. Instead of wasting time and energy hacking at trees, he went to the beach and gathered big armfuls of driftwood. He also collected dried grass for tinder. By nightfall, he had built several roaring fires to keep everyone warm—including the men who had been chopping wood and were now cold because sweat had soaked through their clothes. Kavanaugh had the good sense to choose easily-available materials to make big fires in the shortest possible time.

Stay in Control!

Never forget that fire is dangerous. Lighting a fire in the wild is a big responsibility. Fires that get out of control can do enormous damage to animals, birds, and the landscape. Even a small campfire can leave an ugly scar on the countryside if you don't clear up properly afterward. A true survival expert is always careful to respect the wilderness.

Safety First

Never make your fire any larger than it needs to be. This helps keep it under control and also saves fuel. If you have chosen your site well, there shouldn't be **flammable** materials nearby, such as dry leaves or overhanging trees. However, you still need to keep watch over your fire at all times, just in case.

DID YOU KNOW?

In very dry places, fire can spread underground through smoldering tree roots and break out elsewhere.

Huge forest fires like this one in Greece start easily in summer, when the ground is very dry.

TRUE SURVIVAL STORY

PETER FLEMING was a writer who joined an expedition to Brazil in 1932. One day he saw a distant forest fire and climbed a tree to watch. It was a terrifying sight. The fire raced across the land, creating huge, twisting clouds of smoke. The air was hot and murky, and the sky was full of burning embers that started new fires wherever they fell. Fleming suddenly realized how close the fire was getting and leapt out of the tree as hot sparks burned him. Luckily, he was able to run downhill to a riverbank to avoid the fire.

Overnight Embers

If you want to make your fire last through the night, you need to keep a few embers glowing—but not so many that the fire is in danger of spreading while you sleep.

Let the fire burn down in the evening, then add thick, green sticks that will smolder slowly through the night. Throw on a few handfuls of dirt as well. In the morning, scrape the dirt and ash away, then add tinder and kindling to get the fire going again.

Putting dirt on top of your fire reduces the amount of oxygen that can feed the flames.

Vanishing Act

When you've finished with your fire, make sure it's completely out and that you remove all traces of it.

1. *First let the fire die out. Then rake over the embers to help them cool.*

2. *Pour cold water on the embers to make sure the fire is out. Check that no vegetation or roots nearby are hot or smoking.*

You can then scatter the embers and rake over the site again.

Sod Trick

If you make a fire in a grassy area, first cut out a large square of **sod** and build the fire on the soil underneath. When you put out your fire, make sure the embers are cold and then replace the square of sod. This means that you cover up the scar of your fire completely. After a few weeks the ground will be back to normal and no one will ever know you were there.

◀ *Don't leave your fire site looking messy like this. Rake it and turn over the stones to help them cool down.*

Fire for Cooking

Being able to cook food in the wild is a useful survival skill. A hot meal gives you vital energy and helps keep your spirits up if you are cold or lost. You can also use your fire to boil water and make it safe to drink. But remember, pots and pans get hot over a fire, so don't burn your hands on them.

Getting Started

Choose a flat spot for your fire or stove, so pans or pots don't topple over. If you don't have any cooking utensils, then try making your own (see pages 26–27). Remember that hygiene is just as important in the wild as at home, so wash your hands before handling food, and clean your cooking utensils after using them.

▼ *When your fire has burned down to hot, glowing embers, you can grill food over it using a wire rack like this one.*

Trench Fires

It's a good idea to make your cooking fire in a shallow trench, or pit, away from wind. You could also build a small wall of rocks or logs nearby to reflect heat back toward the fire.

1. *Dig a rectangular trench that is about 1 ft. (30 cm) deep.*

2. *Lay your fire fuel inside. You could also line the trench with flat stones to help retain heat even when the fire has died down.*

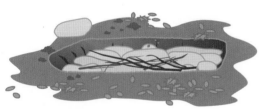

Cooking Stands

If you don't have metal grills or stands for your food, try using materials around you. For example, you could make a spit for roasting food such as fish. You could build a tripod or crane to hang a pot above the fire, or rest a large pan on two logs placed on either side of the fire.

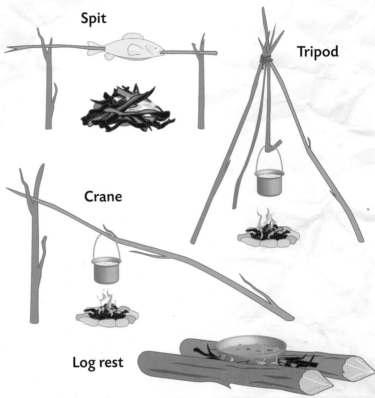

Spit

Tripod

Crane

Log rest

Boiling Water

If you need drinking water, look for fast-moving rivers and streams. This water is less likely to contain harmful **bacteria** than still, **stagnant** pools. Get as close to the source of the river or stream as possible, and check for dead animals and any other pollution in the water. Before drinking the water, boil it over a fire for at least five minutes to kill off bacteria.

▶ *This camel guide in the Sahara Desert is boiling water to drink.*

Cleaning Up

If you clean your pans with dish soap, use a very small amount so you don't pollute the water in the wild. You can buy **biodegradable** dish soap, but even this can still affect the environment. Do your washing in a spot downstream from where you might be collecting drinking water. Store any food scraps in containers out of the reach of animals.

Using a Stove

If you're going on a camping trip, you could take a small stove to cook on. It won't give you much warmth, but it will make cooking and boiling water very simple. Just don't forget to take some fuel!

▼ *This boy is cooking burgers on a camping stove that has plenty of space for heating pots and pans of food.*

Stove Types

There are many kinds of camping stoves. Some stoves burn gas, which is a mix of butane and propane, while others use gasoline, alcohol, or paraffin. Some stoves burn more than one fuel, which is useful in remote places where you might have a limited choice of fuel to buy.

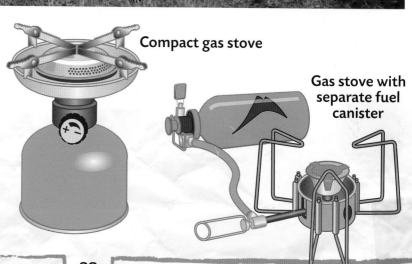

Compact gas stove

Gas stove with separate fuel canister

How Much Fuel?

Fuel is heavy, so don't carry more than you need—but make sure you have enough. The amount of fuel you need will depend on how long you're going away and how much cooking you'll be doing. If you take ready-cooked foods that only need a few minutes to heat, then you can reduce the amount of fuel you use.

Filling Up on Fuel

The method of refueling a stove depends on the type of fuel it burns. With gas stoves, carefully unscrew the empty gas canister and replace it with a full one. If you are using alcohol, make sure the burning container has cooled before you refill it. Be just as careful with paraffin and gasoline. Always refuel away from your tent or shelter. If in doubt, get an experienced adult to help.

▲ A hiker cooks over a compact stove. Placing rocks around the stove helps prevent it from getting knocked over and also keeps the flame shielded from wind.

Stove Safety

Never use your stove inside a tent, as it could flare up or get knocked over. If this happened, your tent could catch fire very easily. Also, just like wood fires, stoves give off small amounts of carbon monoxide and use up oxygen. This means that you should always cook in the open air where there is plenty of ventilation.

◀ This stove was put together from pieces of scrap metal. Food can be put inside to cook, just like in an oven.

What to Cook

There are plenty of specially-prepared foods you can take into the wild. These include canned food and wet pack food, which just need heating, as well as freeze-dried food, which you heat after adding liquid. However, there's a limit to how much you can carry. On long trips, or in emergency situations, you will need to find food from natural sources.

◀ These **Aborigines** in Australia are fishing using handmade tools, including a long, sharp spear used to stab fish.

TRUE SURVIVAL STORY

ERNEST SHACKLETON was a famous Antarctic explorer. On one expedition in 1914, he and his crew faced a long, cramped, cold journey by boat. Their only comfort was their stove, which they used to heat milk and also to cook a thick stew called hoosh. The hot food and drink gave them energy and hope.

Plenty of Plants

There are many plants in the wild that you can cook and eat, but you need to know what you're looking for. Stick to things you know for sure are safe to eat, and only pick fresh, healthy-looking plants. Many mushrooms are **edible**, but unfortunately some are extremely poisonous—and it can be very difficult to tell which are which! To be safe, it's best to avoid all mushrooms.

Simple Soups

Soups and stews are easy to make because you can add whatever you can find. In forests, this might be nettles, dandelions, vegetables, and herbs. In cold places such as the Arctic, you could boil up edible mosses and **lichens**.

▶ *Nettles won't sting you once they're cooked, and they're a very healthy food.*

Tasty Insects

Many insects are very **nutritious** and can be easily roasted over a fire or added to a soup or stew. Ants, termites, grasshoppers, beetles, and worms are all edible. Avoid hairy, brightly-colored or smelly insects, and those that sting or bite.

▶ *Grasshoppers like this one can be baked, fried, boiled, or roasted on sticks. Be sure they are well-cooked, or they could make you ill.*

Fish and Meat

If you're able to catch fish or small animals, make sure they are cooked well to kill any bacteria. A good way of cooking fish is to hang pieces on a log near the fire, and turn them over when one side is cooked. For meat, thread chunks on sticks and roast them.

Fish cooking on a log near fire

Meat and vegetables on sticks

Cooking Methods

You've already seen some simple and effective ways of cooking, such as roasting or grilling meat and fish over the fire. However, if you're in the wild for a long time, you might want a bit more variety in your cooking! Here are a few other ideas for making tasty meals.

DID YOU KNOW?
Romany *people used to cook hedgehogs in* **clay**. *When they cracked open the clay, the spines came off too. Don't try this, as hedgehogs are becoming rare and shouldn't be eaten.*

This man in Samoa is cooking using an oven called an **umu***. Food is placed on hot stones and covered with banana leaves.*

A Good Fry-Up

Frying is great for hungry hikers! Put meat, fish, eggs, or vegetables in a flat pan and rest it on the embers so the food sizzles. You can also make your own frying pan using a large, flat rock. Set it on top of the fire and wait for it to heat up. It's a good idea to add oil or fat to keep the food from sticking to the pan or rock—but be careful, as hot oil can catch fire.

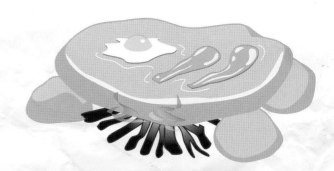

Heated Pits

Try making a heated pit to bake your food in. You need to dig a pit that is about 2 ft. (60 cm) deep and wide enough for the food you need to cook.

1. Heat plenty of big stones in the fire. When they are hot, put them into the pit.

2. Cover the stones with grass or edible leaves. Wrap food in leaves and put them in the pit.

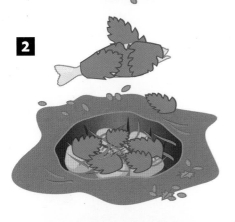

3. Fill the pit with leaves, grass, and soil. Leave the food for a few hours so the heat from the stones cooks it through, and then dig it up. You might need to practice this to get the timing just right!

Baking in Clay

If you are in a place where there is a lot of clay, then you can use it for cooking. Cover your food in clay and put it in the hottest embers of the fire. The clay protects the food from burning, but allows enough heat in to cook it. The only difficulty is knowing when your food is ready. Don't eat it unless you're sure it's properly cooked.

Earth Ovens

Many groups of people, such as **nomads**, who live using traditional ways, build earth ovens. These ovens are usually deep pits or large domes that trap heat to bake or smoke food. Sometimes water is poured on hot stones and food cooks in the steam.

▲ This is an outdoor earth oven built from mud by a group of nomads called **Berbers**. A wood fire heats the oven.

Making Utensils

If you're planning to be in the wild for a long time, you may want to make your own cooking utensils such as bowls, pots, and spoons. The kind of utensils you craft will depend on the materials you can find and whether you have useful tools such as a camping knife. The key is to improvise with whatever you can lay your hands on. Be creative, and keep trying!

DID YOU KNOW?
American Indians traditionally used the stomachs of dead animals as containers for food and water.

▲ *These women in Africa are using huge, hollowed-out **gourds** as water containers.*

Careful Carving

If you have a good knife, you can use it to carve utensils out of wood. Soft types of wood, such as pine and basswood, are good for carving spoons, forks, plates, bowls, and other utensils. Remember to be very careful when using a knife. Always carve away from yourself, and pay close attention to what you're doing.

▶ *These bowls for grinding spices were carved by a craftsman in Puerto Rico.*

Cups from Bark

Tree bark is a useful material for making pots and cups. Use birch, cedar, or elm trees since their bark is softer and more flexible than others. Strip bark from fallen trees or branches, and peel off the rough outer layer, leaving the smooth bark underneath.

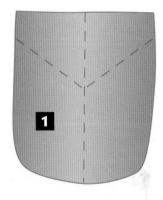

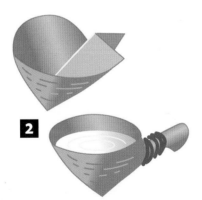

1. *To make a simple cup, cut a piece of bark roughly this shape and score lines as shown.*

2. *Fold the bark along the lines and wrap cord or thick grass around the handle part.*

Clay Pots

If you can find clay in the ground—for example, around riverbeds—then you can make your own clay pots. Knead the clay well to get rid of air bubbles. Then shape your pot and leave it to dry. To make it last longer, you need to heat it. To do this, put it under a layer of soil and build a fire on top. Let the fire burn for a few hours.

Burned Bowls

Try making simple bowls or spoons by burning hollows in wood. Get a good fire going first, as you'll need lots of embers.

1. *Place an ember on a piece of wood. Press it down with a stick and blow on it to keep it glowing.*

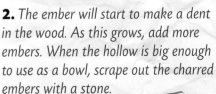

2. *The ember will start to make a dent in the wood. As this grows, add more embers. When the hollow is big enough to use as a bowl, scrape out the charred embers with a stone.*

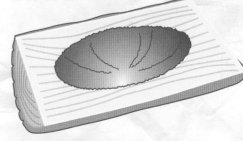

Test Your Survival Skills

Have you learned the skills you need to build, light, and stay in control of a fire in the wild? Would you know how to use the fire for cooking? Take this quiz and find out! You can find the answers on page 32.

1. What three things do fires need to burn?
a) Fuel, oxygen, and heat
b) Tinder, fresh air, and kindling
c) Carbon monoxide, oxygen, and gas
d) Smoke, wood, and matches

2. Fungi, moss, and shredded paper can all make good...
a) Kindling
b) Tinder
c) Food
d) Feather sticks

3. Where's the best place to build a fire here?

4. Which of these trees provides the best wood for burning?
a) Alder
b) Elder
c) Ash
d) Lime

5. You start a fire, but it's really smoky. Why might this be?
a) It's too small.
b) It's too big.
c) You used seed heads as tinder.
d) You used damp wood.

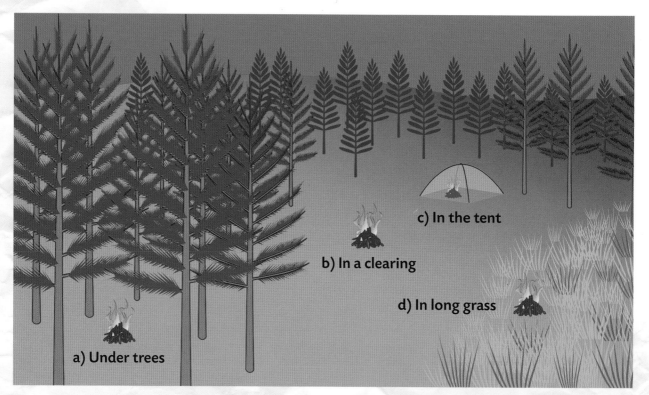

c) In the tent

b) In a clearing

d) In long grass

a) Under trees

6. You're making a stew. You shouldn't add...
a) Grasshoppers
b) Dandelions
c) Worms
d) Mushrooms

7. Where's the best place to use a friction stick to make fire?
a) A hot, dry desert
b) A wet, steamy rainforest
c) A high, snowy mountain
d) A dark, damp forest

8. You're collecting wood for a fire. What's the best fuel here?

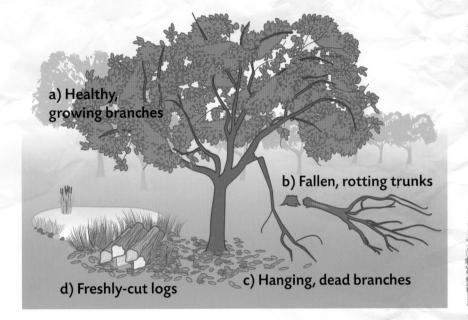

a) Healthy, growing branches

b) Fallen, rotting trunks

c) Hanging, dead branches

d) Freshly-cut logs

9. How long should you boil water to make it safe to drink?
a) Just until it starts to bubble   b) Between one and two minutes
c) At least five minutes   d) At least half an hour

10. Why shouldn't you put wet stones in your fire?
a) They might be slippery.
b) They might contain water, making them crack or explode when hot.
c) They might make the fire produce extra smoke.
d) They might make food taste odd.

11. How is food cooked inside an oven called an umu?
a) Heated by hot rocks
b) Roasted on a bed of embers
c) Fried in oil
d) Boiled in hot water

12. What is NOT a good way of making sure your campfire is out?
a) Raking over the embers
b) Pouring cold water over embers
c) Sprinkling grass on hot embers
d) Checking whether nearby vegetation is smoking

Glossary

Aborigine   A member of a group of native Australian people. Aborigines lived in Australia long before Europeans arrived there, and are traditionally skilled hunters and trackers, with excellent wilderness knowledge.

bacteria   Tiny, single-celled living things. Some bacteria are harmless, but others can cause diseases.

Berber   A member of a group of people from North Africa. Many Berber people live in nomadic tribes.

biodegradable   Able to be broken down or decomposed harmlessly in the environment by bacteria and other living things.

Bushman   A member of a nomadic group of people from Southern Africa.

carbon monoxide   A colorless, odorless, poisonous gas that is formed when certain fuels, such as natural gas, burn without enough air around.

clay   Very fine-grained soil that is easy to mold into shapes when wet, and then hardens when heated.

edible   Suitable to be eaten.

ember   A glowing, hot fragment of wood, coal, or other natural fuel. Embers can start a fire and also remain when a fire has burned down. They are good to cook on since they give off lots of even heat.

fire piston   A device used in the jungle to light fires. It is a hollow tube, often made of bamboo, with tinder, such as dry moss, at the bottom. A wooden plunger fits inside the tube. If you hit the plunger again and again with the palm of your hand, air inside the tube gets so compressed that it heats up and ignites the tinder.

flammable   Any material that ignites easily and burns quickly.

flint   A very hard, grayish-black stone that breaks into pieces with sharp edges. When a piece of flint is struck hard against steel, it creates sparks.

friction   The effect of rubbing one object or surface against another.

gourd   A large fruit with a tough skin. Gourds belong to the same plant family as pumpkins and squash.

green   Wood that is freshly cut from a living tree and contains lots of watery fluid called sap.

hoosh   A thick stew made from pemmican, water, and ground-up biscuits. Hoosh was often eaten by early Antarctic explorers.

lichen   A living thing that is a bit like a fungus. Lichens grow on places such as tree trunks and bare ground. Some look like yellow, crusty patches, while others are bushy growths.

machete   A wide, heavy, sword-like knife that is used for cutting or as a weapon.

nomad   A member of a tribe or group who moves from place to place with herds of animals.

nutritious Something that contains lots of nutrients, which are the natural substances your body needs to work properly. Nutrients include vitamins and minerals.

oxygen A colorless, odorless gas that makes up about 20% of the air around us. We need oxygen to breathe.

pemmican Shredded, dried meat that has been pounded into a paste, mixed with fat and shaped into strips. Pemmican can last for a long time if it is stored properly, so in the past, it was often used by explorers as an emergency food.

pollute To contaminate with poisonous or harmful substances.

prairie A treeless, grassy plain. Prairies are found in central areas of the United States and Canada.

precipice An overhanging or extremely steep mass of rock, such as a cliff face.

Romany A member of a group of people who live mainly in Europe, but came originally from India. Romanies are often known as Gypsies.

sod The top layer of grassy ground that consists of grass, matted roots, and soil. If you have to build a fire on grass, it's best to remove a section of sod with a knife, then replace it afterward.

stagnant Water that is still, without any flow or current, and has therefore lost its freshness and become stale.

taper A thin strip of wood, paper, or other material that is used to transfer a flame.

tar A dark, sticky substance that is produced by the burning of natural fuels such as wood or coal.

tepee A cone-shaped tent, traditionally used by American Indians. A tepee fire is one that is built up in a cone shape.

umu A type of earth oven from Samoa. Food is covered in leaves and buried among hot stones to cook. More leaves are then piled on top to make sure no heat escapes. Umus can be big enough to cook whole animals, such as pigs, and are often used for special occasions such as traditional feasts.

Useful Web Sites

http://www.wildernesscooking.com/index.html
Tips, menus, and recipes for cooking while on backpacking and canoeing trips.

http://www.wilderness-survival.net/chp7.php
How to build a fire based on information from the U.S. Army survival manual.

www.wildwoodsurvival.com/survival/fire/index.html
Read about all the different ways of making fires.

www.woodcraftwanderings.org
Find out lots of bushcraft information, including how to build a fire and make cooking utensils.

Index

Answers to survival skills quiz (pages 28–29)

1a, 2b, 3b, 4c, 5d, 6d, 7a, 8c, 9c, 10b, 11a, 12c